Snap out of it!

25 Choices
To Be Happy

Debbie Gisonni

Snap out of it!
25 Choices To Be Happy

For Information:
Real Life Lessons, LLC
PMB #396
1017 El Camino Real
Redwood City, CA 94063-1632
www.reallifelessons.com

Author Cover Photo by Joe Prestipino

ISBN: 0-9744909-0-3

Printed in the United States of America

To Joe and Angela, who can always make me laugh,
and to Sydney, who really cracks me up!

Contents

Choose Acceptance

It's so easy to accept the good stuff when it happens to us. We savor those fortunate moments like a rich, slow melting piece of Godiva chocolate caressing the tongue. But when we're faced with bad news or unpleasant feelings, we fight, ignore or deny them like the plague. We dig in our heels and think, *"Not in my lifetime is this going to happen!"*

There is a generation of people who experienced more than the usual death and loss, while they struggled through WWII and the great depression. Having gone through so much pain, they seem to be more accepting of what happens in their life. My parents were part of that generation. After my mother became disabled, she would often say, *"I never imagined I'd be living like this."* Then in the same breath, she'd follow with, *"I guess it's God's will."* Whether it was God's will or not, the acceptance of her uncontrollable misfortune helped her stay sane through ten consecutive years of chronic illness, disability and near death experiences.

Now, I'm not suggesting you roll over and play dead when life deals you a bad set of cards. You should always attempt to change and improve whatever you can. But sometimes, a tornado sweeps into your life without cause or warning. While you can't prevent it, you can certainly live through it. That means acknowledging it and adjusting your life to accommodate and embrace it—without anger or guilt. Major setbacks are often lessons that help you change your life for the better.

Death is one of the most difficult events in life for us to accept. Often family members choose to deny a terminal diagnosis or worse, assume they're doing the dying person a favor by not telling him. Then the person dies without the opportunity to say good-bye, make amends or get his affairs in order. Afterwards, the remaining friends and family are left with an even larger burden—sorting out the mess *and* all their emotions of denial. They may never accept their loved one's death, which can cause a domino effect of emotions from anger to hate to depression. On the other hand, had they accepted the impending death, they might have been able to make that person's last days more joyful and their own less frustrating.

By accepting the events in your life, you accept life itself. You become more tolerable of others and more content with your personal situation, whatever it may be at the time. You realize that every event in your life—trivial or life changing, fortuitous or tragic, eventually comes to an end.

Life will always be a series of ups and downs. For some of you, it's a roller coaster ride. For others, it's just a few bumps on a rather flat road. Either way, you'll be happier if you hold on, pay attention and embrace every bit of the ride.

Five ways to choose acceptance in your life:

- Say and believe each morning that you are open to whatever the day brings.

- Consider death a natural part of life—talk about it, work through it.

- Remember that unhappy events and emotions are temporary—don't deny them, they'll come back to haunt you.

- Embrace misfortune; it will make the good times feel that much better.

- Don't worry or blame yourself for things out of your control—go with the flow.

Choose Adventure

When I was thirty-eight years old, I walked into a tattoo shop with a drawing of a sun, moon and star to be etched into my ankle. It was like a rite of passage for me after leaving my fifteen-year career. I had willfully jumped off the corporate treadmill and traded it for a time of emotional upheaval, financial challenges and yes...adventure. I had no idea where I was going or how to get there, yet the anticipation of new possibilities was exciting. Some friends and colleagues thought I was insane to leave a successful career, but I listened to a voice inside me that beckoned like a blinking lighthouse to a ship in a misty fog. It said, *"Do it, do it, DO IT."*

It was that same voice that encouraged me to move three thousand miles away from home when I was twenty-three and elope at twenty-six. These decisions were not the most popular with my Italian-American parents—OK, they were devastated by my actions! After all, they believed in making safe choices in life, just like they did. A conviction guaranteed to render a life of unhappiness, just like theirs.

My parents discouraged adventure as a way of protecting me from disappointment. As a child, I felt like a dog behind an invisible fence. Each time I was tempted to go beyond the line, I felt a shock to the back of my neck, usually in the form of my father's voice saying, *"What are you— an idiot? You'll kill yourself doing that!"* Thankfully, there were more times in my life when my spirit of adventure outweighed the memory of my father's advice. Even if it was only to show him that not everyone who skis breaks a leg! And if I did (break a leg), at least I was doing something I enjoyed.

Adventure is having the courage to take risks in life without the anxiety of being judged negatively or failing. If Columbus cared about his reputation, he would've played it safe and stuck to the theory of the flat world. And who knows when someone would have discovered the medical benefits in bread mold. How dull life would be without adventure!

As for that tattoo I wanted, I did get it a few days later—*after* I had obtained a prescription for an analgesic cream. No need to include pain in my adventure!

Five ways to choose adventure in your life:

- Take the path in life you want, not the one others expect you to take.

- Turn fear into excitement by visualizing the best outcome of a risky decision.

- Commit to trying something new—food, sport, class—twice a year.

- Don't listen to naysayers; they're secretly jealous of adventurers.

- Change a familiar routine—route to work, morning ritual, Saturday lawn mowing.

Choose Balance

For years, the media has led the charge on the importance of balancing work and life. I not only believed it was the key to happiness, I was convinced that I had it all under control. I worked in the high paced, high stress world of high tech, and even as I was climbing the corporate ladder of success, I still managed to eat healthy, exercise daily, entertain friends, remember birthdays and take vacations. Then when my family started to fall apart due to illness and death, I successfully lived two separate lives with the skill of a juggler watching one ball in the air and one in the hand. One life was in and out of corporate boardrooms doing business presentations, and the other was in and out of hospital rooms dealing with doctors.

I looked as though I had effortlessly achieved what most women strive for their entire lives—balance. But the only thing balanced about my work and life was that they both provided an equal amount of daily stress. I was continually feeding my physical self (my ego) with the lists I finished, the sales I exceeded or the meals I perfected. The more my ego got fed, the more my spirit was starved. As I continued to increase my responsibilities at work, the line between who I was and what I did completely vanished.

When my health started to suffer, and my mind started to wander, I walked away at the peak of my career. I did not consult part-time. I did not take another job. (I did not pass GO and collect $200!) There was no middle ground that would get my equilibrium back. I was too far out, like a fishing line tangled in a bed of muddied seaweed. The only solution was to cut the line and start over. That's when I embarked on a whole new life and work journey that was truly balanced—nurturing my body, mind and spirit.

Companies will be bought and sold. Work will come and go. This is the temporary nature of the physical world in which we live. The key to balance in life is creating harmony between the spiritual world we come from and the physical world we live in.

Five ways to choose balance in your life:

- Take up a hobby that has nothing to do with your job.

- Feed your spirit regularly—meditate, get a massage, exercise, write, paint, sing.

- Don't be connected to work twenty-four hours a day, just because you can.

- Socialize with people outside of work, including family, friends and pets!

- Never miss, postpone or cancel vacation time.

Choose Change

During the 1980s, when I was leading teams of sales people in the high tech industry, I remember a familiar cliché I once used to begin a sales presentation: *The only constant we can depend upon is change.* Even in the fast-paced, ever-evolving environment of technology, people resisted change. It was so much more comfortable and safe to hang on to what they knew. It was, and is, human nature. Holding on to the past— regardless of whether it was painful or glorious—is like swimming upstream with cement shoes. You'll eventually sink to the bottom, hopelessly fighting the natural current of life—unless you choose to lose the shoes and point your feet downstream.

When my family was hit with tragic illness, all I wanted was my perfect life back. Before the hospitals and nursing homes. Before the battles with doctors and insurance companies. Before the rancid smell of sickness and grinding noises of life support. After a while, I realized I had three choices. I could live in the past and be angry over the events that had fallen upon my family. I could live in the future and worry about what terrible thing could happen next. Or, I could adapt to my new life and accept each day as it came. I had no control of these changes that leapt into my life, including the four subsequent family deaths that followed. However, I did have control over how I chose to embrace them or not—making them a part of my life, not something that was happening outside of it.

No day is exactly like another. We're constantly challenged to adjust in a changing environment. Some of those changes are small, and we manage them without a thought—a delayed meeting time, a cold, a rainy day. Some are huge—a death, a marriage, a move. Either way, they are all just moments. Moments that dissolve into new moments. Nothing is permanent. Your house, your car, your jewelry and your money are merely props given to you to help you navigate through life.

These too shall pass. You don't know when. It could take a lifetime or just a day, but once you accept the impermanence of life, you also accept that anything can vanish in a moment, including your own life.

It's impossible to prepare for unexpected changes, but when they come (and they will), you should welcome them and learn. Regardless of whether these changes are joyful or devastating, they will always advance you to another step on your life's path. Thankfully, life continues to happen. If you can adapt with it, your journey will be much happier.

Five ways to choose change in your life:

- Live in the present moment; it's the only place you can affect change.

- When something bad happens, ask yourself what you can learn from it.

- Accept that any plan you make may change.

- Be open-minded to other's attitudes, opinions, and ways of doing things.

- Stop trying to control everything that happens in life—you can't.

Choose Connection

Can you imagine those peer-pressured, awkward years in high school without someone to talk to—a best friend, a sibling or a radical aunt? Ironically, that's the time when you're most centered on yourself, and yet it's precisely when you need to connect with others. I used to worry about everything—my clothes not being hip enough, my curly hair not staying straight on a rainy day, my parents not finding out about the boy I met at the dance. It was all about me! But without my friends, in whom I confided my daily dilemmas, I would have drowned in a sea of my own self-doubt.

While there is an inherent emphasis in our society on individuality, our path in life is not meant to be traveled alone. The connection you make with others, whether they are friends, family or strangers, is what gives your life meaning. With the exception of some religious orders, in which monks vow to live in solitude, most of us need other people (or at least a pet) to add texture to our lives. Studies show that social connections have a positive effect on our well-being.

Some say the Internet is the ultimate connection for everyone in the world. The Internet cannot, however, replace companionship, because it disconnects you from emotions and spirit. Email can never replace the spectrum of emotions created by the physical interaction with another human being. The Internet will not teach your children how to listen to the sound of a voice with their hearts or how to hug a friend who is hurting.

The connections you make during your time on earth are like a million lifelines floating in a vast ocean—each with its own unique life preserver, only a thought away from embracing you. When your world is turned upside down and you want to crawl into a shell, the best thing you can do is reach out for one of those lifelines. All it takes is your desire to connect.

Connecting with others is nourishment for your soul as much as food and water are for your body.

Five ways to choose connection in your life:

- Make small talk with a stranger.

- Research your family tree and call a long lost relative.

- Join a group that meets regularly—a social club, meditation group, parents group, sports team.

- Phone a friend you don't see often—rather than sending an email.

- Spend quality time with your family.

Choose Diversity

Americans often take pride in the fact that we have a diverse population consisting of different races, religions and nationalities. One would assume an environment such as this would encourage and celebrate the differences among us. Why then does our multi-cultural society often make us feel ashamed to be different?

Aside from my looks (olive skin, dark hair), much of my ethnicity growing up was defined by the food I ate. As a child in grade school, I remember being singled out and embarrassed by classmates for the lunch my Italian immigrant mother used to pack for me. Crushed meatballs or pepper and onion frittata stuffed into a thick hunk of Italian bread gave a whole new meaning to the brown bag lunch. Once I opened the olive oil stained bag, the smell of garlic and onions permeated the entire lunch room! Inevitably someone would ask me, *"What is that?"* The tone of those three little words made me yearn for a plain bologna or peanut butter and jelly sandwich on white bread.

Today I appreciate all that sumptuous ethnic food, not only for the taste, but for the fact that it was the cornerstone of my family's cultural rituals—the 1:00 p.m. Sunday afternoon mandatory pasta meal, the 6:00 a.m. aroma of garlic and onions simmering in olive oil, the sizzling roast leg of lamb (not turkey!) on holidays. I now consider myself lucky to have eaten frittata instead of bologna for lunch, and for being exposed to foods many of my American friends never had the opportunity to try.

I don't believe America is as much of a melting pot as it is a nation of people with unique differences—some of which have been borrowed from each other and assimilated into the American culture. Funny how we are so quick to demand diversity in everything we consume—from the food we eat to the flowers we plant to the cars we buy. Yet when it comes to the category of people, we want everyone to be the same. What an absurd and boring concept! We all come into this world with our own special qualities—the color of our skin, the food we eat, sexual preferences, religious beliefs, personality. No one should ever feel left out, embarrassed, or even worse, killed for being different.

Imagine what your school years might have been like if all the kids accepted each other's differences. No fights, no bullies, no embarrassment. Now think of that concept on a broader scale. What would happen if we required the families of people at war to spend a week living together, learning about each other and peacefully exchanging cultural rituals, food and conversation? Maybe they would figure out that they are much more alike than different, because they share the most common bond there is—that of the human race!

Five ways to choose diversity in your life:

- Take time to learn about and appreciate different cultures through books, documentaries, magazines, travel, foreign language classes or cooking classes.

- When you meet people who are different from you, welcome them into your circle, ask them about their culture, and be open to talking about yours.

- Stop judging people immediately after looking at them.

- Stop judging nations of people only by what the news media reports.

- Plan a monthly trip to your nearest big city, even if it's just to walk around.

Choose Faith

One of my all-time favorite movie lines comes from the 1947 version of *Miracle on 34th Street*. It was recited by both lead actors, John Payne and Maureen O'Hara—*"Faith is believing in things when common sense tells you not to."* There have been questions in my own life that I can only surrender to faith. *"Can I have a financially sustainable career doing what I love? Will I always have good health? Am I really doing what I'm here for in life and work?"* While I have some days laced with tension, fear and worry, I try to overshadow them with faith that everything will turn out OK. I have no material evidence to support this belief. I just trust that it will.

I believe that we are all spirits in earthly form, and that there is a higher power or creator in whom I place my trust. But regardless of what your religious or spiritual beliefs are, or if you have any at all, you can still have faith. Faith is a trust that you place in custody or care of another. Even if you don't believe in anything beyond your own physical reality, you still have someone in which to trust—yourself. You cannot deny your own existence.

When I was in the business world, I needed very little faith to make things happen. I knew that I could successfully execute most any plan I put into motion. I knew that if I did A+B, I would get to C. After I left the corporate market and entered the world of book publishing and writing, I initially embarked on my mission exactly the same way as I would have done in business. First, develop a business plan with objectives, budget and timeline. Then, execute that plan diligently and efficiently. Finally, obtain desired results. After four years of planning, executing and a lot of hard work, I realized that A+ B was not getting me to C. No matter how focused and passionate I was, things just didn't work out exactly as I had planned. Yes, I had pretty lofty goals, but that never hindered my success in the corporate world. After a while, I felt defeated. I was physically and emotionally worn out. Though I had accomplished much, I wasn't nearly where I wanted to be. I couldn't *make* anything happen using the same skills and logic that had served me well in business. So, I did the only thing I could to keep my sanity. I gave up control to faith. Instead of focusing on what I hadn't achieved, I started believing in all that was still possible. I trusted the universe would never leave me hanging on a thread for my next meal, and what was supposed to happen would happen at exactly the right time.

And so, I continue to write...

Five ways to choose faith in your life:

- Believe in miracles, especially those involving you.

- Regularly initiate conversations with God, angels, fairies, your higher self or any such spirit entities.

- Don't be attached to our earthly definition of space and time.

- Imagine what it feels like to have a certain thing happen and keep that feeling for a minute each day.

- Use positive thoughts and words when envisioning the future.

Choose Forgiveness

Have you ever made a mistake? Of course you have. We all have!
If you were the only one affected by the mistake, you might just
consider yourself foolish. If it caused harm or inconvenience to another
person, you might apologize. Either way, you need to make one last
choice—to forgive yourself or not.

We often talk about forgiveness as it relates to forgiving others, but
forgiveness starts with ourselves. Of all the prejudices and stubborn
opinions we harbor, we save the most judgmental and condemning for
ourselves. *"I should've, could've, would've...I can't get anything
right...I'm no good."* Even for the smallest infractions that shouldn't
warrant a second thought, like eating that piece of chocolate cake that

wasn't on the diet, we refuse to forgive ourselves. We abuse our self-worth every day by never giving ourselves a break.

If we're not accustomed to forgiving ourselves, it's difficult to forgive others. By holding on to hate and blame for the people who harm us, it may make us feel like the keepers of justice, but all we're really doing is stoking the coals of a dangerous fire burning within us. A fire that destroys love and humanity. While justice and the law should prevail, the human heart needs to heal each time an infliction is made. Fire won't heal it—only love and forgiveness will.

When my younger sister committed suicide in her early twenties, I imploded with guilt. I hated myself for not being able to prevent it, and I hated my sister for causing my family so much pain. Then I hated myself even more for hating her! The months following her death were filled with depression, anxiety and a depth of sadness so dark that I felt like I was living in a thick black cloud of smoke, smoldering in its putrid fumes. I finally decided to see a family counselor. After a couple of months, I was able to rise above the cloud of darkness, but only after I forgave my sister and myself for our mistakes. I learned that I couldn't continue to blame myself for another person's actions, and that forgiveness instantly lightens a heavy heart.

Each experience you have in life is a lesson, especially those that are most damaging to you. You can't predict or know what someone else's lessons in life are, and therefore, you can't judge them for what they might do—even if they hurt you. Once you forgive yourself and others, you can let go of the pain *and* the past.

Five ways to choose forgiveness in your life:

- Find the lesson in your mistakes and then move on.
- Apologize when you've hurt another person.
- Know that all people are capable of love, even though their actions say otherwise.
- Know that forgiving a person brings peace of mind for oneself.
- If a person causes you emotional pain, tell them.

Choose Generosity

When my father was alive, I was always acquiring pieces of his wardrobe—mainly robes, flannel shirts and hats. He was the type of person who would gladly give away all his worldly possessions, though he didn't have much. If a friend was fond of something of his, he would say, *"Here, take it. It's yours!"* without expecting anything in return. He wasn't particularly attached to material things, so if it could make someone else happy, he'd give it away.

Sometimes the people who are the least fortunate financially are also the most generous. It seems that the more you have, the more you want to *keep* what you have. You become too attached to the material world and forget about all the people in it.

Most gifts are given out of guilt or obligation. We toss them back and forth for holidays or birthdays, like a grass stained softball that's waiting to be caught by a person who feels it's rightfully theirs. Even charitable gifts can become more of a duty than an act of love. When I was growing up, my church dictated that ten percent of the family's income should be donated to the church. When donations were low, they were quick to remind us by devoting an entire sermon to the subject. And so, people gave out of guilt *and* in fear of being denied at the gates of heaven!

True generosity, however, comes from the heart and can take many forms—money, gifts, love, compassion, physical assistance, time, food, services, advice, or even an open ear. When you give unconditionally, it's like releasing thousands of molecules of love and compassion into the universe that attach themselves to people, places and events. And, if you give anonymously, those molecules multiply exponentially!

Whatever you put out in this world comes back to you tenfold. It may not come back in the same form you sent it, but the universe will surely reciprocate, in some shape or form, in this lifetime or the next.

When I receive a gift, I can feel the love that surrounds it. It makes me happy and thankful. When I give a gift, I feel the same love, because that person's happiness and gratitude is *my* gift. Giving *is* receiving, and receiving *is* giving. They are one and the same.

Five ways to choose generosity in your life:

- Give someone a gift, just because.

- Don't brag about what you give.

- Never expect anything in return for your generosity.

- If you think someone could use some help, offer before they ask.

- Each morning, ask yourself how you can serve humanity—then do so.

Choose Gratitude

One of the first things I remember learning to say was *"thank you."* It didn't matter how small the gift or deed, I can still hear my mother's voice ringing in my ear, *"What do you say, Debbie?"* Those two simple words can be more beneficial to the psyche than years of therapy. Why? Because when you thank someone from your heart, you make that person feel appreciated, loved and relevant. Isn't that what we all want out of life?

Sometimes it takes a tragedy to remind us to be grateful. After my mother's operation to remove a brain tumor, the doctors told us she would be home in six weeks. She subsequently spent three consecutive years in hospitals and nursing homes. Ironically, the anger and self-pity we felt in the first year was later replaced by gratitude. Years of hospital visits revealed countless families dealing with illnesses much worse than my mother's. We became thankful for our own fate, as bad as it seemed at the start. We also became grateful for life, particularly my mother's since she lived another ten years after her surgery. Even in the most difficult times, there's something for which to be thankful.

Everything in life is a gift. Just think of the food you ate today. As small and insignificant as an apple may seem, there were many people involved in putting that apple on your table—the farmer who grew the tree, the worker who picked it, the trucker who transported it, the store owner who displayed it. Those are just a few people you can thank for that apple! And while you're at it, add nature to the mix— sunshine, rain, birds, insects, etc. They all played a part in that one little apple. How lucky you are to have all those forces joining together just for your personal nourishment.

How many times have you had an opportunity to thank someone or God today... but didn't?

Five ways to choose gratitude in your life:

- No matter how bad a day you have, think of one thing for which to be thankful.

- Say *"thank you"* to people as often as possible…and mean it.

- Send "thank you" cards or notes after receiving dinners, gifts, parties, hospitality, advice, friendship, and business.

- Thank your children for being in your life and teach them the value of gratitude.

- Think of all those people who would trade their lives for yours in a second.

Choose Humility

Enough about you, let's get to me! Me, me, me...it's all about me!
Being in front, first and recognized is highly encouraged in our society.
We place more value on humiliation than humility, because we think
standing out is better than staying within. Just watch a few minutes of
any reality show, and you'll see how easily people volunteer to trade
public humiliation for fifteen minutes of fame.

Between my first and second book, I had a rough time—
emotionally, physically and financially. I had yet to be recognized
nationally for my work (Oprah wasn't calling!), my husband was in
between careers, and a back injury prevented me from writing. One day
I was caught in a traffic jam on my way to an appointment in San

Francisco. I got increasingly frustrated sitting there as my mind started replaying all my problems. By the time I got into the city, I was depressed about my career and my life. I kept thinking about poor little me.

As I drove through the city, I saw the familiar sight of street beggars at each intersection. Most of them were men—some sitting on cardboard boxes, some with signs asking for money. One after the other, I passed them without stopping to give them anything. There was a mantra I grew up with in New York about the homeless that goes something like this: *"Don't give to beggars on the streets. They'll only buy alcohol or drugs with the money. Donate to organized charities instead."*

As I got to the end of a long line of intersections, I stopped at a red light and noticed a young woman a few feet in front of me begging at the corner. She couldn't have been more than eighteen years old with long straggly dirty blond hair, a petite chiseled face and piercing light blue eyes. I could see the outline of her ribs through her mismatched ragged clothes that hung from her emaciated body. Her bony arms were wrapped around a cardboard sign that said, *"Please help. I need food and money."*

The driver in front of me handed her a can of soda, and I watched while she strained a smile to thank him, as if her face muscles could barely command the skin to move. I quickly started rummaging through my purse, hoping the light wouldn't change and cause the drivers behind me to start honking their horns. I whipped out a $5.00 bill and gently handed it to her, smiled and wished her a good day. She said thanks and continued walking to approach the car behind me. I immediately wanted to give her more, but traffic had moved on, and I was already on my way. Driving back through that same intersection later that day, I looked for her. She was gone.

All I could think for the rest of the day was how humble that woman was. She sought the light in others, without realizing it was actually her own light that attracted them to her. That was when I knew that my life was about a lot more than just me and my own little problems.

Five ways to choose humility in your life:

- Know that as soon as you think you're humble, you're not.

- Imagine yourself living someone else's life, less fortunate than you.

- Let others shine, and be happy for their success.

- Give others credit when they deserve it and sometimes when they don't.

- Stop talking and boasting about yourself and listen to what others have to say.

Choose Humor

What would you think of me if I told you I had an uncontrollable laughing fit at my mother's funeral? Yes, it really did happen! Knowing it wasn't socially acceptable, I tried to suppress it, but after a while, I felt like a balloon that was holding too much air. When I finally let it out, I had a tremendous emotional release. I guess my subconscious chose laughing over crying that day. Given a choice, I'd much rather laugh.

Sometimes the most difficult circumstances in life provide us with the most humor—if we're open to it. During a time of long-term family illness and multiple tragedies, I remember many moments of laughter amid all the sadness and grief. I realized that when things got bad, my family could always find the funny side of pain, because we were used to laughing at ourselves—from my mother's crazy, mixed up Italian/American/Brooklyn accent to our own clumsy falls. So when my mother was hooked up to a respirator and couldn't speak, we had no trouble playing a humorous alphabet game to communicate with her. When she lost her gag reflex and couldn't eat, we made funny faces mimicking her as she sung her daily vocal exercises, which consisted of ten minutes of ear piercing sounds.

From a very young age, we are taught to be responsible, which often translates into being serious like adults. We become experts in drama, but never really learn the ins and outs of comedy. Have you ever been around someone who can laugh at her own shortcomings, find humor in any situation, and make you laugh as well? Those are people with a unique talent and gift to humanity. They help lighten the load in life and work by showing you a more balanced, less serious perspective.

I remember a scene from TV news (you know…the messengers of gloom and doom) during the coverage of the September 11th tragedies. It was a clip of hundreds of frantic people running to escape the falling rubble from the crumbling World Trade Center. A reporter stopped one man whose face was covered in black ash. His hair was disheveled, tie undone, shirttails hanging out. As the reporter asked for his comment, the man started to smile, almost chuckling to himself, as he answered, *"I'm sixty-four years old, but I can still run like I'm sixteen!"* Despite the horrific tragedy happening behind him, he was able to find one grateful thing to laugh about.

As you struggle with life on earth, magnifying and internalizing all of your problems, listen to your higher self. I'm sure it's telling you, *"Lighten up, already!"*

Five ways to choose humor in your life:

- In a terrible situation, look for isolated moments that are funny by themselves, regardless of the bigger picture.
- Give yourself permission to laugh, and have fun every day in any circumstance.
- Watch comedies on TV and film, and appreciate the masters at work.

- Don't take yourself, your ego or job too seriously; they can all be gone tomorrow.

- Try to get a baby to laugh—watch and listen to how funny you can be!

Choose Innocence

We often associate innocence with young children—those who are pure and uncorrupted, blameless of any wrongdoing, incapable of feeling guilt. When we use innocence to describe an adult, however, its meaning changes to someone who is clueless, uninformed, ignorant or unsophisticated. Why is that? Do only children have the right to be innocent? Today even that right seems to be taken away as we rush our children into schools immediately after toilet training, expect them to speak like adults, compete in sports, excel in academics and behave responsibly—all because these are the ways we define success in our society.

Even as a child, I was never a child at heart. From about age nine and on, I was a very serious kid—always analyzing, worried and disciplined. I felt like the weight of the world was on my shoulders, or at least the weight of my family. On the outside was a smiling, skinny petite girl with dark curly hair. On the inside was a twisted rope that willfully tightened with intensity around my next chore, homework assignment or outfit choice for the following day. I worried about my family. I wanted us to have enough money. I wanted us to all get along. I wanted us to be happy. Contributing to this fastidious sense of responsibility was an underlying Italian Catholic upbringing that revolved around guilt—the antithesis of innocence. While innocence makes anything possible with just a thought, guilt usually cancels the notion of that thought!

Innocence is your natural state. It is how you are born. (Clearly I don't believe in the original sin theory.) It is you without the burden of guilt about things you said or didn't say, did or didn't do. I don't believe God ever intended us to have such man-made, manufactured guilt that lingers on and on. Remorse for a wrong doing, maybe, but even that is

44

meant to be followed by self-forgiveness, so that we can move on with our life.

Being innocent is not ignorant. It is knowing all there is to know at this very moment.

Five ways to choose innocence in your life:

- Keep your thoughts and actions focused on the present moment.

- Bury your regrets; nothing can change the past.

- Have a conversation with a three-year-old.

- Don't do or say anything out of guilt.

- Forgive and forget at all times.

Choose Integrity

We all grow up with a set of experiences and lessons that shape our value system and create our foundation in life. I grew up in a lower middle class immigrant family. For the most part, my parents set a good example as honest, hard working people who always did the right thing. I'm not saying we were perfect. I had a godfather who did small favors for the mob, and a mother who frequently acquired salt shakers and handfuls of sugar packets from restaurants! Despite that, my parents must have done something right, as I've never had the urge to swipe anything off a restaurant table.

In housing construction, the stuff that holds the foundation together is called mortar. In life, that mortar is called integrity. Similar to houses, foundations in life can either start with cracks or develop them later. Even if you grow up in the perfect Beaver Cleaver household, things happen in life that cause stress on your foundation. Like a house settling as a result of gravity and bad weather, your life settles as a result of situations—divorce, neglect, fear, abuse, peer pressure, work stress, illness, poverty.

Cracks in your foundation may cause your integrity to waver. People who grow up poor may feel pressured to steal to make ends meet. People who were abused as children may not be emotionally capable of breaking the cycle of abuse with their own kids. People who weren't loved may think they can only find love in gangs or drugs. While you can't change the foundation created by the environment in which you grew up or the subsequent life events that follow, you have a choice to fill in the cracks with love and to learn from them, or to use them as an excuse for immorality. That's why two children who grow up in the same exact household can take their lives in entirely different directions—one fills in the cracks, the other chooses to widen them. It's all about free will.

And just for the record—so you don't think every Italian-American is part of the mob and enamored by "The Sopranos"—my father immediately cut off all communication to my godparent's family as soon as he got word of my godfather's activities with organized crime. I've never seen or heard from them since.

Five ways to choose integrity in your life:

- Set an example for those around you—always tell the truth.

- Take responsibility for any wrongdoing.

- Don't buy anything from someone who cheated or stole to get it.

- Pay back personal loans, even if it's just a dollar.

- Don't keep anything that isn't really yours, including praise.

Choose Joy

What is joy to you? It can certainly take many forms. For one person, it may be the sound of children laughing or the smell of puppy breath. For another, it's dancing in the moonlight or eating ice cream. For yet another, it could be a soothing massage or a free-style parachute jump.

We often associate joy with the things and events in our lives that produce the warmest and fuzziest feelings of pleasure deep within our soul, but true joy requires no stimuli. It's a state of mind that exists regardless of what's happening around you. You can access joy even during the most painful times in your life, because you have a place for it inside of you (which can be found), and a memory of it (which can be reproduced). It's like going to the automatic teller machine and making a withdrawal for happiness. But unlike your bank account, there's an unlimited supply of joy to receive and share!

In my family, food always brought us much joy—preparing it, eating it or talking about it. I remember a story my father used to tell me about a time when he was away from home in the Marines. One day, a package arrived from his mother containing a homemade blueberry pie. He was so excited that he and his comrades skipped the utensils, broke through the flaky crust with their hands, and shoveled the gooey mixture into their watering mouths. There was a look of sheer joy in my father's eyes each time he told that story. Later in his life, when he was dying of bone cancer, I personally carried a homemade blueberry pie on a plane from California to New York, just to see his face light up one last time. Even when people are dying, you can bring a little joy into their life…and yours.

When people ask me how they can find happiness during difficult times, my answer is always the same: It's a matter of choice. Joy is present in your heart at all times. It's your choice to use it and your privilege to share it.

Five ways to choose joy in your life:

- Recall a happy memory and focus on it long enough to bring back the feeling.

- Laugh, smile and joke whenever and wherever you can.

- Call or see an upbeat friend.

- Take a break from TV news and violent shows.

- Stay away from negative or angry people.

Choose Love

Have you ever asked yourself, *"Why am I here?"* This is the question that has titillated the minds of historians, theologians, and the entire human race since the beginning of time. Often, we're looking for a very complicated, deep and mysterious answer, but after we peel away all the layers of social conditioning, peer pressure, religious dogma and media standards that we've been exposed to since birth, the answer becomes quite simple. It's LOVE! We're here to learn to give and receive love—unconditionally.

There are many ways to show or feel love in life. For example, in my home growing up, love was expressed through food. My Italian parents had a hard time saying the words, *"I love you,"* but I still felt loved (at least most of the time) in the way I was nurtured and comforted with delicious food. Even as an adult, when I came back home to visit, my mother always managed to have my favorite meal ready for me, despite the fact that she had become disabled. I knew how much effort it took for her to make that tray of eggplant parmesan, and I truly appreciated and enjoyed every bite of it!

With the plethora of self-help books and tapes available, we've all heard the expression: *You must first learn to love yourself before you can love others.* While most of us aren't ready to stand naked in front of a mirror admiring ourselves, it's important to start somewhere (maybe an earlobe), so that you can begin to love not only your physical attributes, but everything about you. The way you talk, act and feel—imperfections and all. Self-love also means forgiving yourself for any misdeeds or harmful thoughts.

Once you start the process of loving yourself, you open the door of reverence to all life—people, animal, plants, situations, nations, earth. You choose to replace hate and anger with love, because you know that harming another (emotionally or physically) is incongruent to life. Even if someone has harmed you, love allows you to forgive that person. There are true stories of people who have forgiven their attackers, sacrificed their life for the safety of another, given when they had nothing to give, or helped a stranger in need. All of these are acts of unconditional love.

Your collective thoughts, words, actions and emotions create the environment in which you live. If you choose love over hate, love is what you will bring into your life and into the world. You'll feel good about yourself and others and live a more happier, peaceful and meaningful life, knowing that love is *all there is*.

There is no power in the universe greater than the power of love.

Five ways to choose love in your life:

- Find something, no matter how small, to love about yourself and tell yourself every day. Build this list with time.
- Send loving thoughts to all people or situations you dislike.

- Consider yourself and all human beings to be the children of God—perfect in every way, no matter how we outwardly appear to be.

- Vow never to harm another person—emotionally or physically.

- Extend all of the above to the animal and plant kingdom, and remember to be thankful for those that you consume.

Choose Now

Whenever I watch my dogs lying around, I can't help but wonder what they're thinking, or if they're thinking at all. We humans tend to spend a lot of time thinking. Mostly about what has already happened or what we think might happen, rather than what is happening right now. Even as I write this, I'm thinking about how I'm going to cook the salmon for dinner later this evening. All this time spent in the past and future leaves little or no time for the present, which is the only time that really matters.

I've lived most of my life hurrying to get to whatever was next on the agenda. Even as far back as grammar school, I could remember memorizing all the answers in the *Highlights* books, so by the time I was in 3rd grade, I was reading the 5th grader's edition. I don't know why I was in such a rush to finish. Certainly, no one was pushing me to advance at that pace; however, I did receive kudos for doing so. On the other hand, by barreling through the lessons so fast, I didn't learn much of anything—or at least anything I could remember the next day.

This pattern would continue well into my adult years. For example, I had no desire to sink my teeth into college culture when my only goal was to graduate, so I doubled up my classes and finished early. That got me an extra year in the—oh so fun—New York City commuter rat race. Then in business, I became one of the youngest women in the high-tech industry to run a magazine. That got me an all-consuming job, an eighty percent travel schedule, and an education on what *not* to do for personal health and wellness. Looking back, it's all a big blur of images, like sticking your head out the window of a speeding car. I was moving too fast to notice the scenery along the way or to enjoy the journey. I only remember the final destinations.

Sometimes it takes a catastrophe to force you to stop and be present. When you have to drive your car through a heavy snowstorm, you can't help but pay attention to every bump and slide. Normally, you're driving in auto pilot, while your mind is working overtime. *"How late will this traffic make me? I need to pick up Ryan from his basketball game. What am I making for dinner?"*

Life is in its most perfect state when you are present in every moment. Living in the past or future, as we often do, only serves to drain your spirit. You can't change what has happened, nor can you worry about what hasn't happened yet. So, instead of living in the land of *"I could've, should've, would've"* or *"what if,"* try living in the land of *"I am,"* because *now* is the only moment you can affect and enjoy.

Five ways to choose now in your life:

- Stop and notice every detail in the backdrop of your daily life—color, smell, people.
- Savor each moment in life. Like snowflakes, no two are the same.
- Good or bad, keep the past in the past.

- Stop worrying about what you can't change or don't know.

- Concentrate on one thing—whatever you're doing or saying at this very moment.

Choose Optimism

Have you ever wondered where the expression, "knock on wood" comes from? There are several theories dating back to the Pagans, Christians and ancient Celtics. The most common is that knocking on a tree woke the good spirits who would protect people from evil. Today's version includes knocking on any wood-like surface, but the premise remains the same—preventing bad luck. To me, it's just another form of negative thinking—focusing on the bad instead of the good.

You bring into your life that which you focus upon. If you're one of those people who thrives on gloom and doom, yanking others into your web of despair, and then gloating about your foresight when life becomes as miserable as you feared—guess what? This becomes your own self-fulfilling prophecy! You will always live in victim mode, shunning happiness, while you anticipate your next inevitable misfortune.

Amid these forces of negativity, notice that there are others who always seem cheerful, finding the good in any situation or person. The words, "Murphy's Law," never touch their lips! You may think that they have all the good luck. And they do! Because they focus on how great things are or can be, versus what can ruin it. And, if something does go wrong, they find the lesson in the experience—maybe even the silver lining—and move on positively. These are the people who choose optimism.

When I woke up one day to find my car tire flat in my driveway, I didn't think, *"These things always happen to me. This car has been bad luck since I bought it."* Instead I chose to think, *"Wasn't I lucky to have this happen here, instead of while I was driving 60MPH on the freeway?"* OK…you say, *"Big deal! It's just a flat tire. What about the really bad stuff that happens to us, like death, divorce, bankruptcy, illness?"* My answer stays the same—*How you see it is still your choice.* I lost four family members in four years, and my mother was ill for ten years. After that devastating time, I decided to write a book to help others deal with tragedy. I wanted to turn those tragedies into something positive for others and myself. That was my choice.

Optimism is a learned behavior. If no one in your life has ever taught you to be positive, then it becomes your choice to learn. You create the reality around you with your thoughts, words and actions. It's the law of the universe—what you put out, you get back. Simple. Negativity zaps so much energy from you and comes back ten times stronger. It's cold, dark and heavy on your soul, while being cheerful and optimistic feels like a cool summer breeze—light, sweet and airy. Try it sometime; you may never go back.

Five ways to choose optimism in your life:

- Hang around positive people even if it seems uncomfortable at first.

- If you work or live with negative people, don't get pulled into their fear or impose your opinion upon them.

- Try to change every negative thought and word to a positive one.

- Always assume the best from people and situations.

- Make positive affirmations—if you say it enough, you'll start believing it.

Choose Participation

If life were a pair of jeans, what would yours look like at the end of

your life? Would they be worn and faded, thinning in spots, soft to the

touch with the hem unraveling? Or, would they be crisp and clean, stiff,

tags still on them with perfect creases, vibrant color and pockets intact?

If my parents had their way, mine would be the latter. I was raised with

what I call a "life saver" mentality. No, not the candy. The kind of

environment where couch cushions were covered in plastic and never

touched by human flesh, bathroom towels were only for show or

company, money was saved and only spent on necessities, new clothes

were never worn right after you bought them, entire rooms in the house

were not used, and the only lit candles were on birthday cakes or in church.

Today I make a point of lighting all candles in my house, allowing them to burn instead of collecting dust. I usually line up about a dozen candles in my fireplace—all different sizes, colors, fragrances and shapes. Then I light them all and become mesmerized by the dancing flames that look as if they're playing a well-orchestrated piece of silent music. Just like the unique direction each life takes, and the variety of experiences that await us, no two candles melt the same way—some drip slowly like sap on a tree; some widen their walls like the mouth of a cave, exposing their shimmering light; and some collapse inward, engulfing their flame like molten lava. A half-melted candle is like a wise middle-aged person who has enjoyed and savored life—a person who is not afraid to continue to ignite the flame of life until there is nothing left but a tiny piece of metal that once held the cord to its existence.

Too often we save things in life for the wrong reasons. We save our emotions because we don't want to be hurt, our appearance because we don't want to look messy or old, or our flaws because we don't want to be anything less than perfect. All this saving prevents us from fully participating in the journey of life. We become a bystander in our own life, worrying about what is gone or already melted, instead of focusing on the new experiences that are being illuminated for us.

Allow the flame of life to entrance you, burn you, titillate your senses, soften you. Participate in life and you'll have more fun than you ever imagined!

Five ways to choose participation in your life:

- When you have a rainy day, use what you saved for it.

- Don't hold back your feelings, especially those of love and compassion.

- Don't believe you're too old to try something new—sport, adventure, love, hat, hair style.

- Every now and then, allow your kids to jump up and down on the bed and then join them.

- Use all your material possessions and share them with others; you can't take them with you when you leave this earth.

Choose Passion

Have you ever watched a musician perform? I'm not talking about just listening, but really watching their body movements and facial expressions? Once I saw a Santana concert on TV. I've always loved their music, but on that evening, as the camera cut to each band member's solo, I was watching rather than listening. I started to notice how their personas transformed while they were singing, drumming or playing the guitar. Their faces contorted to the beat of the music, heads cocked from one side to the other, eyes closed—looking within. What I saw for the first time was how much passion Carlos Santana and his band members had for their music. It was as if they *became* the music. They were no longer performers on stage; they were music and soul, joined as one.

When my husband decided to give up his eighteen-year career in high tech, he considered photography (a life long interest) as a new venture, but his logical mind didn't feel at ease with it. So I asked him some questions. *"How does he feel when he walks into a camera store and sees all that equipment and beautiful photography displayed? Does he feel like a kid in a candy store? Does he love the smell of it? Does he want to stay forever? Does he even get a little excited?"* His answer—*"Yes! Yes! Yes to all of it!"* OK, maybe he didn't admit to getting excited, but photography was his passion, and to be true to himself, he needed to pursue it.

Passion is a feeling that comes from deep within your heart like a bubbling caldron of hot liquid. You can try to put a lid on it, but the steam escapes every now and then, reminding you of what is just beneath the surface, feeding your soul. Most of us have a passion for something in life. Maybe it's spending time with your children, skiing or watching old movies. It's what gives you joy. It's what brings a smile to your face.

You can always tell if people are passionate about something just by listening and watching them talk about it. Their faces light up and eyes twinkle, as if there's a current of electricity swirling inside them. Some people seem to have that electricity within them all the time. Those are people who truly have a passion for life. When you meet them, you think, *"I want some of what she has—that energy, that joy."* You can readily have it. Find passion in everything you do, and you will enjoy even the most mundane or stressful moments of your day.

Passion allows you the freedom of creativity without the burden of logic.

Five ways to choose passion in your life:

- Send loving thoughts to every task, person or situation.

- At least once a week, do something you love for an hour.

- Join a group with similar interests as yours.

- Notice what makes your heart flutter, and do more of it.

- Share your passion with others. (If it's knitting coasters, give them away as gifts; if it's music, perform free at a friend's party.)

Choose Patience

While growing up, patience was one of those qualities I would put in the category of "do as I say, not as I do." My father used to fly off the handle if any small thing went wrong, especially if it involved fixing something around the house. In traffic jams, he would immediately turn off the radio and start muttering curse words in Italian (his native tongue). My mother was no better. She hated to wait for anything. When summoned by her, I was expected to come running instantly—no questions asked. She also did everything at lightning speed—a trait I'm sure I inherited from her. (We vow never to be like our parents, but we often become replicas.)

Watching parents and their children interact provides great

examples of either patience or impatience. Not having children myself, I'm sometimes in awe at the incredible amount of patience that parents can have. I commend my sister, Angela, for trying to teach her daughter, Sydney, about patience at a very early age. When Sydney was about two years old, she entered that demanding two-year-old phase, where she wanted what she wanted, when she wanted it, and that was NOW! Angela would calmly tell her that she had to be patient. Then she would ask Sydney if she knew what patience meant. Sydney would reply, *"No,"* and Angela would explain that patience meant to wait a minute. After a while, Sydney started to remember the answer, and when Angela said, *"You need to be patient. Do you know what patience means?"* Sydney would reply, *"It means wait a minute."* After that, if she stopped whining for a while, she would get rewarded. It became a little game that gave my niece the attention she wanted, while also teaching her something.

We often go through life like a two-year-old child. We're not willing to wait for anything, whether it's as trivial as our turn in line at the supermarket or as serious as our life-long dream. How many of you get frustrated when the driver in front of you is just going the speed limit? When you have to listen to a friend who tells long, boring stories all the time? When you need to save money before buying something? While we all strive for instant gratification (hence our huge credit card debt), if we were willing to wait a little, instead of pushing all the time, our lives would be less frustrated and more content.

Usually, things happen in life at exactly the right time. Have you ever thought that the extra five minutes at the automatic teller machine, waiting behind someone who obviously can't read or push buttons faster than a toddler, might save you from being at an intersection just at the moment when someone decides to run a red light? It sort of makes waiting look like a blessing.

Five ways to choose patience in your life:

- Daydream about pleasant places or memories whenever you're waiting in line.
- Send loving thoughts to anyone trying your patience.
- Listen and evaluate a situation before you speak or act.

- Stop looking at the clock every five minutes.

- Be thankful for a delay; it could save your life and/or create an opportunity.

Choose Peace

When I was young girl, I loved watching beauty pageants, especially when they got down to the last few contestants and the big question at the end. It seemed that no matter what the question, *"world peace"* was the right answer. I truly believed those dazzling women would someday make the world a better place!

I was only three years old when the Vietnam War started in 1964. It wasn't until 1969 that I started to understand what was going on. At eight years old, I willingly did my share for the peace movement. I drew peace symbols all over my homemade schoolbook covers right alongside my flower power stickers. I didn't know anyone in the war, but I did catch enough to know that people were dying and many were missing in action. I never knew how my parents felt about the war—they never talked about it in front of us—but when my sister and I asked for POW/MIA bracelets, they didn't hesitate to buy them for us. I proudly put my shiny metal bracelet on every morning and carefully placed it upon my dresser each night. In the evenings, I'd say a prayer for my guy, and during the day, my friends and I would search through the list of found POW and MIAs in the newspaper. We used to chat about our guys as if they were family.

At that time, I had no comprehension of the political backdrop for the war or who was winning, nor did I care. The only thing that mattered to me was the safe return of my guy and all the guys over there, wherever "there" might be. Children have a natural ability to cut through the illusion created by adult egos and see what really matters in the purest sense. I knew that people were being killed and that homes, villages and the earth were being destroyed. I knew that was wrong.

After the Vietnam War was over, I stopped wearing my bracelet. It had become dented and scratched over the years—the name barely visible. I kept it in a box on top of my dresser until I left home at twenty-three years old, eleven years after the war had ended. I never knew if my guy ever came home—alive or dead.

When asked, most of us say that we want world peace. A good place to start is within oneself. Peace doesn't come from a country or a political leader. It begins with you being at peace with your body, your spirit, your life. Then and only then, you can bring peace to others—from family to friends to strangers to community to country, and finally to the world. As human beings, we all come from the same source of pure love, and that's what connects us in spirit. By killing another, we kill a part of ourselves—the human race.

While I don't watch beauty pageants anymore, I do give the contestants credit for knowing that Peace *is* the only answer.

Five ways to choose peace in your life:

- Always respect others' beliefs, opinions and actions, especially when different from your own.
- Hold the image of world peace in your heart and mind, feeling it every day.

- Detach yourself from the mob mentality, created by the media to stir your emotions into seeing only one point of view.

- Choose the path of least resistance—walk away from arguments, fights, negative people, explosive situations.

- Meditate or pray daily to create inner peace.

Choose Silence

For a couple of summers during high school, when I didn't have an early job, I woke up to the familiar sounds of my mother cooking, my father and sister leaving for work, and my younger sister playing. I used to stay in bed after everyone was gone just listening to the silence of the house. As the rising sun splashed upon my lime green bedroom walls (hey, it was the 70s), I felt so peaceful and happy. I would lie in bed and soak up the silence. It was the only time during the day my mind wasn't cluttered with the noises of the external world.

Those summer mornings were long forgotten once my adult career was in full swing. Being still, even for a moment, seemed unnecessary, and even more so, detrimental to the constantly moving treadmill of life

and work I ran upon. I needed to keep doing at all times. *"Do, do, do,*
because if you stop, you'll fall off and lose your place in life!" In our
technologically advanced culture, filled with stimuli to keep us going
twenty-four hours a day, there is no encouragement for silence or
reflection—unless you're a three-year-old child in time-out! Most of us
shun silence, opting instead to spend our time alone, drowning in the
constant din of the TV.

After I left my corporate job, I spent a lot of time doing nothing.
Then I decided to start meditating. Yes me…the person who used to
wake up in the middle of the night and leave my staff voice mails.
Meditation allowed me to practice silence, and once I did that, it wasn't
long before I was able to rekindle the feelings of those peaceful
mornings in my teen years. In meditation, I truly began to understand
what I was here on earth to do. It's amazing how you hear the most
profound things in silence.

You can find silence anywhere—in a raging crowd or in a quiet
forest. Just imagine being connected to both the center of the earth
below you and the Creator of the universe above you. All it takes is a

little practice and commitment.

Five ways to choose silence in your life:

- Join a weekly meditation group, or start one on your own.

- Create a ten-minute daily ritual (upon waking or before sleep) for prayer, meditation or silence.

- Turn on the TV to watch something—not for background noise while you're busy doing other things.

- Take a walk in nature.

- Practice doing absolutely nothing.

Choose Simplicity

I remember studying Maslow's hierarchy of human needs in high school. It seemed pretty simple. Once our basic needs such as food, clothing, shelter and security were met, we start advancing up the pyramid to three more levels: social needs (love, entertainment, community), self-worth (ego satisfaction, recognition), and finally, self-realization (personal/spiritual growth, contributing to mankind). Chances are, you're somewhere in the top three tiers of the pyramid. If you're like most people, you're stuck in the gridlock of self-worth, because the ego doesn't like to be left behind. It often grips us like a fierce undertow, keeping us under its power, wave after wave. This is a by-product of our rich American culture—proving our self-worth by the things we have. While we should buy and do things that bring us pleasure, we should also enjoy what we have, even if it's just a little.

Several years ago, a friend's daughter came into my house and said, *"Your house is so small. How do you live here?"* She lived in a much larger house and upscale neighborhood. Even though she was just a child, her comment gnawed at me like a fly buzzing around my ears. I started thinking that maybe we did need a bigger abode. Then I thought, *"Had I become so ego conscious that I needed my house to impress a ten-year-old child?"* I wanted to slap myself in the face and yell, *"Snap out of it!"* While I chose not to cause myself personal injury, I quickly reminded myself how much I loved our home and how perfect it was for us. I didn't need anything more.

Knowing the difference between needs and wants is the first step to simplifying your life. When I was a child and wanted a new dress, my mother would ask me, *"Debbie, do you really need it?"* Most times I didn't. It's difficult to simplify our lives when we succumb so easily to pressure from commercials, friends, family and yes…even children. *"What would they all think if I don't have the latest, greatest, biggest?"*

If you keep your purchases to 50% needs and 50% wants, you'll live a pretty modest life. If you slide the scale to 80/20, you'll simplify even more. Anything below that will probably have you living in a tree house!

Living a simpler life allows you to use and enjoy everything you have. And, if you happen to have a lot of money and like spending it, you could always help or treat others. Maybe then you'll finally reach that self-realization tier.

Five ways to choose simplicity in your life:

- Maintain existing cars, houses, and appliances—buy used when possible.

- Don't live for your mortgage—find a smaller home or less expensive area.

- Don't live on credit only—buy what you can truly afford.

- Trade money for time, and always choose time!

- Ask yourself the need/want question before buying anything.

Choose Surrender

I've hated surprise parties ever since my mother threw me one for my sixteenth birthday—an age when the last thing you want to do is party with your mother and her friends. I never encourage visitors to drop by my house without calling first. And God knows, I would never allow the success of a dinner party I'm giving to be contingent upon what guests bring...or don't. Call me a control freak (I prefer to use the term, "Type A personality"), but I like things to run smoothly and as planned. I can't help it. I was born Type A, all the way. Driven to succeed, no matter what the challenge. Organized, productive and reliable. Always in control. For that, I received much praise and acceptance from my family, friends, teachers and business colleagues.

All of this adoration, of course, only encouraged me to become even *more* efficient. How great to be in complete control of my own destiny! Whether it was the next job I wanted or my next day's outfit, I planned and executed each with the same intensity and drive. Like a hungry cheetah chasing a gazelle, there was nothing stopping me from point A to point B.

Then life threw me a couple of unexpected curves. People in my family suddenly got cancer and brain tumors, and one even killed herself. All outside of my control. That sense of security and control I had built my life upon was instantly proven non-existent—a mirage between my mind and reality. It took a while for me to figure out that there are scenes on this grand stage of life that are impromptu and uncontrollable. During those times, the only healthy thing to do is to give up control and surrender.

Some of us need to hit a brick wall (or two) before we finally surrender that sweat gripping hold we have on every outcome in our lives. If you're set on a particular goal and can only see one path to get there, you're cheating yourself of happiness that can come in unexpected ways. You become a 6'5" brawny bouncer blocking the front door of a night club called "unlimited possibilities." You always have that option to move away from the door and see what comes in and out. If you choose not to exercise that option, you may end up getting trampled in the battle between your will and your life.

It is only when you surrender control of your life and of the lives of others that you truly become empowered. When my will is bruised and battered, I naturally loosen up the reigns of control, mainly because I have no energy left to fight. That's when I believe in miracles and dreams that come true with just a wish, not a plan. But please, no surprise parties!

Five ways to choose surrender in your life:

- Consider unexpected change or tragedy to be an opportunity to learn and a gift to grow.

- Be open to multiple ways of reaching a goal, even those you haven't thought of yet.

- Believe that everything happens for a reason, even if you don't know why. Just let it be.

- Take a day off from lists and plans, and see what happens. Go with the flow.

- Don't force your opinions or beliefs upon another person.

Choose Touch

Remember your first crush and how the slightest brush of his or her shoulder on yours would make your racing, pounding heart feel like it was going to break through your body at any second? That's the power of touch! There's plenty of research that confirms the benefits of touch—from babies who are held more becoming better adjusted in life to how a simple hug can actually make a person feel better. A well-meaning, loving embrace immediately creates a positive emotional response by balancing energy and calming nerves.

Who among us doesn't like the soothing strokes of a Swedish massage? I not only enjoy a good massage, I tend to touch and feel everything around me. I love how silky fabrics, smooth marble, velvety flower petals or furry dog ears feel on my skin. I'm the person who walks through a store and touches all the merchandise—just to feel the texture and awaken the senses. (Museums are not a good place for me!)

The human touch can have a profound and comforting effect on people who are ill or dying, and yet these are the people that we often refuse or forget to touch. Let's face it; illness can be ugly. It ravages the body from the inside out. It's already uncomfortable to be around someone who is suffering, let alone touch them. While a mother, a spouse or a sibling may be able to see beyond swollen faces, emaciated bodies or hanging tubes, the rest of us usually try to keep our distance. Have you ever had someone take a step back from you as you were talking to him? How did it make you feel? If you're like most of us, you probably thought you were boring the person to death or that you had bad breath! Either way, you felt rejected. Magnify those feelings by a thousand and you'll realize how someone feels who is sick and *knows* that they look or smell terrible.

When my aunt was dying of breast cancer, her body was burned and bloated from chemotherapy and radiation. I visited her often and sat on her bed just close enough to chat, but not to touch. Then one day, she asked me to rub lotion all over her. I knew I didn't feel comfortable running my hands along the scabs and bruises on her skin, but I gladly obliged as I was happy to be able to do anything that made her feel better. I'm not sure I would have thought of it on my own, but she only had to ask me once. After that, each time I saw her, I went straight for the lotion.

Five ways to choose touch in your life:

- Hug and kiss your children, not only as babies but as they mature as well.
- Look beyond what you see in the sick and touch them; they need physical connection to survive.
- Embrace a person in sadness or grief, if they're acceptable to it.
- Indulge in therapeutic body treatments and massage.
- Hold hands with your partner.

About the Author

Debbie Gisonni spent fifteen years in business sales, marketing and executive positions, leading and motivating teams of people through major product and company changes. She was one of the youngest women to become publisher of a multi-million-dollar magazine in the high tech industry. After a series of family tragedies, Debbie founded Real Life Lessons® in 1998, a media and consulting company dedicated to personal well-being, spiritual growth and business success. Her mission is to inspire people to be happy and prosperous through positive changes in life, business and home.

Debbie is the author of the inspirational memoir, *Vita's Will: Real Life Lessons about Life, Death & Moving On,* and the column, *Be*

Happy. She produces information and business advice in various media formats and presentations.

Debbie has been a guest on numerous radio and TV shows across the country, and is an experienced speaker who has addressed audiences of all kinds—from corporate to women's groups to teens. Her articles have appeared in *The San Francisco Chronicle, Simplycity, Living in Balance, Nonprofit World* and more. She is co-editor of *Bookwoman* (the national newsletter for the Women's National Book Association) and volunteers her time for other non-profit organizations.

Originally from New York City, Debbie now lives on the West Coast with her two biggest passions in life—her husband and dogs. Other passions include, but are not limited to, people, physical fitness, roller blading, skiing, biking, walking, writing, cooking, food, painting, tarot, furniture design, interior design, feng shui, dance, drumming, all kinds of music, and laughter.

For more information about Real Life Lessons, additional products or Debbie Gisonni, please visit www.reallifelessons.com.